W9-AER-486

WITHDRAWN

Also by James L. White

Divorce Proceedings   1972
A Crow's Story of Deer   1974
The Del Rio Hotel   1975

THE SALT ECSTASIES

POEMS BY JAMES L. WHITE

ᴛʜᴇ sᴀʟᴛ
ᴇᴄsᴛᴀsɪᴇs

GRAYWOLF PRESS   1982

Some of the poems in this volume previously appeared in the following magazines: THE CARLETON MISCELLANY: 'The Arc-Welder's Blue.' DACOTAH TERRITORY: 'The Clay Dancer,' 'Summer News.' FLOATING ISLAND: 'Sunday Snow.' GILTEDGE: 'Dying Out,' 'Returning.' HOLY COW! PRESS (*Brother Songs* anthology): 'The First Time,' 'Making Love to Myself.' IRONWOOD: 'Skin Movers.' KANSAS QUARTERLY: 'Submission to Death,' 'Submission to Time.' THE OHIO REVIEW: 'Naming.' THE PARIS REVIEW: 'The Salt Ecstasies.' PEMBROKE MAGAZINE: 'Gatherings.' PRAIRIE SCHOONER: 'Submission to Pain,' 'Vinegar.' SONORA REVIEW: 'Syphilis Prior to Penicillin.'

The author expresses his heartfelt thanks to the Bush Foundation of St. Paul, Minnesota for their generous grant which allowed him time to complete the manuscript.

Publication of this volume was made possible in part by a grant from the National Endowment for the Arts, and in part by generous donations to Graywolf Press.

Library of Congress #81-82140

ISBN 0-915308-31-2
        0-915308-32-0 (paperback)

First printing, 1982

Published by GRAYWOLF PRESS, Post Office Box 142, Port Townsend, Washington 98368.

CONTENTS

9   An Ordinary Composure

11   Gatherings

16   I'd Trade These Words

18   Lying in Sadness

19   The First Time

20   Making Love to Myself

22   Taken to a Room

23   Summer News

24   The Salt Ecstasies

25   The Clay Dancer

35   Skin Movers

36   Overweight

37   Poems of Submission

42   Syphilis Prior to Penicillin

44   Oshi

46   Returning

47   Sunday Snow

48   A Colored Girl

49   Dying Out

50   Vinegar

51   The Arc-Welder's Blue

52   Naming

for Kate Green

Whosoever liveth with these scars
shall dwell outside the camp.

Leviticus

AN ORDINARY COMPOSURE

I question what poetry will tremble the wall into hearing or tilt the stone angel's slight wings at words of the past like a memory caught in elms. We see nothing ahead. My people and I lean against great medical buildings with news of our predicted death, and give up mostly between one and three in the morning, never finding space large enough for a true departure, so our eyes gaze earthward, wanting to say something simple as *the meal's too small: I want more.* Then we empty from a room on Intensive Care into the sea, releasing our being into the slap of waves.

Poems break down here at the thought of arms never coupling into full moons by holding those we love again, and so we resort to the romantic: a white horse set quivering like a slab of marble into dancing flesh.

Why remember being around a picnic table over at Brookside Park? We played softball that afternoon. My mother wore her sweater even in the summer because of the diabetes. Night blackened the lake like a caught breath. We packed things up. I think I was going to school that fall or a job somewhere. Michael'd go to Korea. Before we left I hit the torn softball into the lake and Michael said, 'You can't do that for shit James Lee.'

Going back I realized the picnic was for us. It started raining in a totally different way, knowing we'd grow right on up into wars and trains and deaths and loving people and leaving them and being left and being alone.

That's the way of my life, the ordinary composure of loving, loneliness and death, and too these prayers at the waves, the white horse shimmering, bringing it toward us out of coldest marble.

GATHERINGS

1. New Light

I've been dying to go back
through dust, hymns, and the photos of death.
The Union Station sleeps like a defunct whale
and I join its echoing space to think of caskets settling.
I've returned to dust where the peeling signs read:
REMEMBER ALL DEPARTURES ARE CHANGEABLE
BE SURE YOU ARE IN THE CORRECT TIME.
I want to sleep now
in an afternoon dream pushing 'now' away to die completely
as stone or heart
or rising wind.

I want to dream beyond this aloneness,
to feel him carry me through the wind that is rising.
My father in his white strolling suit.
I ride his shoulders into the greening
light of this damp time.

We take flowers in the morning,
my father, bold as God,
mother in her withering step,
in her withering white,
and me in boyhood with a sword of lilacs.

In this dream my people live forever.
We carry the flowers of waltzing light
into a rising wind, through into spring.

We, who are going on a trip.

2. Memorial Day

'Memorial Day, 1940, Logansport, Indiana.'
is written on the decayed photo I keep.
'Estell, Rose, Roscoe,
Marie by the Hudson with *the boy*.'

They tell me to wave to my aunts
though I don't know what wave means.
I stare like a sullen disease into the camera
with my pale hand floating upward, locked
in that motion forever—
my old man's face like a hospital fart
my ribs mean as a prediction of collapse
my burnt eyes questioning the graves
my mother in her withering cotton
my father's strolling suit.

And because nothing is ever answered
I think of lizards going into the earth
and know like the knots of my back
what anguish lay ahead for us
and stare at that anguish
and stare at nothing at all.

In these small years I stay near my mother
who smells of Lily of the Valley and damp earth
so unlike the men who open life with their blazing shares.
My mother binds vision, silence and pain in her flesh,
and I know in her small turning that all our measured ways
throb toward death.

My aunts are in their eternal black,
placing peonies and little flags on the graves.
I wave to these women, not knowing the word.
Women whose casket lids have long since closed them
into perfect darkness.
Still, my little boy's hand
holding them above ground forever
waving, waving over their graves.

3. Losing Light

'Wave good-bye now, we're going!'
I don't know what going or good-bye mean
and twist my face into a screw.
I leave a place I can't remember
except for an awakening spring
and a river veering near a graveyard perhaps.

We enter the Indianapolis Union Station
early in the evening.
Last sun pours through the corroded windows above us,
lighting the filthy terminal.
My father is slightly drunk and quiet.
My mother is breathless
and I know we are all dying in the train calls,
the old picnic basket and brown paper bags.
I know we are all dying there.

4. Lost Light

Shall we.
Shall we gather at the river.
My mother and father laugh in the early evening
and I know the dream is nearly ended.
. . . at the beautiful, beautiful river.
They rise in lines of kindly light skyward, toward the sun,
at the beautiful, beautiful river.

I wake in lost light
to hear doors echo above the failed day,
and wear the absence
like an old ticket saved for home, though not returning.

I wake and cannot find the river,
nor can I even remember the beautiful, beautiful river.
I've traveled long enough to be old from this,
from seeking the river, the beautiful river.
I cannot find the river, the beautiful river,
or the beautiful way home.

I'D TRADE THESE WORDS

I'd trade these words on the spot
to see you again
in the cold practice room above the city.
Old madame what's-her-name playing for class.

My God Marina, it's you at the *barre*
with old leg-warmers and fine perfume!
I'd trade these words
to be a soundless angel again
pulling my muscles into music.

When too much has gone shabby in my life
I can still see you
so many years after your Achilles tendon
exploded on the Spanish tour,
so many years after my legs stopped jumping.

Do you remember that night after work
we went out with your husband?
We'd done 'The Waltzes Noble and Sentimental'
and it ended with my head resting on your breast.
Your husband and I were like two suitors
with the same lover.
He suddenly touched your cheek
and in that awkward silence I thought,
'I know you more.
I know your body more.'
We had sung the space together

with our design to break each
audience's heart as finally as our own.

What I wouldn't give for that cold practice room
and me lifting you without regard
goddamn it, perfectly
into our timeless air.

for MARINA CHAPMAN DOYLE

LYING IN SADNESS

Moon to my earth come from some other space
so totally white at our evening meal,
wearing a coat that will not last the year,
I love you completely as salt.

Tell the one about an hour before darkness
in your room above the Bangcock Massage Parlour.
The one where pain rises with the bread,
filling you with its yeasting smell.

It's dark.
You exhale a fist of memory.
I love you like weathering wood
in a room of empty pianos.

When you return to something you love,
it's already beyond repair.
You wear it broken.

THE FIRST TIME

Sometimes I'm their first.
Sweet, sweet men.
I light candles, burn the best incense.
Make them think it's some kind of temple
and it rather is.

Like this guy who hauled parts for a living,
whatever the hell that means.
He was like caught light through glass,
and so the candles and the incense.
What would you do with a new colt?

He touched my body the way shadows fall
from an old subject he'd buried,
and he looked at me without fear.

Sweet guy.
So sweet I became really shy and hot
so I had to move easy.
Wouldn't you?
What do you do when it's someone's first time?
I try to clean up my act.
Make it into a first rate number
so he knows he's been with someone.

We're bunglers when it's really good:
bow legs, pimply backs, scrawny chest hair,
full of mistakes and good intentions.
And it doesn't have to do with women.
They're fine too.
Just some understanding between two men.

MAKING LOVE TO MYSELF

When I do it, I remember how it was with us.
Then my hands remember too,
and you're with me again, just the way it was.

After work when you'd come in and
turn the TV off and sit on the edge of the bed,
filling the room with gasoline smell from your overalls,
trying not to wake me which you always did.
I'd breathe out long and say,
'Hi Jess, you tired baby?'
You'd say not so bad and rub my belly,
not after me really, just being sweet,
and I always thought I'd die a little
because you smelt like burnt leaves or woodsmoke.

We were poor as Job's turkey but we lived well—
the food, a few good movies, good dope, lots of talk,
lots of you and me trying on each other's skin.

What a sweet gift this is,
done with my memory, my cock and hands.

Sometimes I'd wake up wondering if I should fix
coffee for us before work,
almost thinking you're here again, almost seeing
your work jacket on the chair.

I wonder if you remember what
we promised when you took the job in Laramie?
Our way of staying with each other.
We promised there'd always be times

when the sky was perfectly lucid,
that we could remember each other through that.
You could remember me at my worktable
or in the all-night diners,
though we'd never call or write.

I just have to stop here Jess.
I just have to stop.

TAKEN TO A ROOM

Taken to a room with you asleep,
I want to touch you there
beneath the galaxy of star quilt.
You unfold letting me into the warmth
and everything rises from my dick to my breath
saying we are here.

In my mind I kiss you away, your beard
and earring, the tattooed heart of Christ
on your chest, and remember
a prison boy named Rubio,
then I kiss down on all of you.

Now I'm taken to a room fully awake
and warned my imagination is out of hand.
They show me a solo screaming bed
and quilt of fallen stars.
I pant hard over this poem
wanting to write your body again.

In this totally conscious poem
you're gone and they unplug my systems,
my heart, my lungs, my brains.
In front of the crowd they flash blinding lights
on my crotch and neuter me down to a smile.

I try to think about your eyes
and remember nothing.
Now they drag me off to the next room
where the real work begins.

SUMMER NEWS

Transients loiter in downtown parks with
the stillness of foxes.
One smiles as if I know him near a fountain
in his center of light,
wearing a faded shirt like summer news.

His body invites conversation.
They threaten tornados through the city as
hunters and prey agree on common shelter.
The storm enters our skin gathering
as we begin the familiar gestures.

In his room I speak of death, its promise of ending.
He undresses me, telling me how tired I am,
that friends have brought me their truths all day.
He seems as beautiful as I wish my life was
in the boiling light of our slight sweating.

Now the old blues
before the bad gin and storm.
We vow total selfishness
and we begin to touch

and we begin to rain . . .

THE SALT ECSTASIES

Salt me down where love was
on a blue burn to remember the real pain.
I'm worn out from my back's arch and pull,
bending like a crazy-house mirror to suit your needs
in this endless flesh revolt, trying to win
with my mouth and ass.

I want to be your yoke this time,
pushing you away in the dusty light
from gutting me to nothing, and stay
drawn in, like an old girl
after a hard Saturday night, her body
empty of carriage,
alone and complete
in the room's stillness.

I leave you first in sleep,
my breasts, my V, and hair,
then take the early bus to Laurel
away from the raw and nameless.

Some farm kid presses against my leg.
I look at the long backs of men in the fields
and doze to dream you're going through me
like winter bone, your logs of arms pushing
me down into some stifling contract with flesh
until I break free for air.

THE CLAY DANCER

1.

You are buried in so many places
like the scattering of diseased ivory.
The infamous motels of quick nights,
the way you like it and do it best.

The *Morning Star* says you didn't sleep well into spring
and finally gave everything away on blue paper
like the hunter's bow and ashes.

He wakes, touches himself there, looks
at the skin magazine and can't sleep.

2.

Toward the last
they said voices summoned you
to write two or three poems a day.
Did you mention the white rooms near Clairmont
or the black roses poised against the stone?
    'No.'

Then what did you write of?
    'The manner of summer suns.
    A walker to spring.
    The false myths of my bloodlines.'

Then what did you write of?
    'How I failed as a man
    or what was asked of my manhood,
    through the long distance,
    dreaming wrong.'

Then what did you write of?
    'Trains under my sleep to Dearborn and beyond.'

Then what did you write of?
    'My first time
    in that hot room.
    The guilt, the shame making it perfect.'

Then what did you write of?
    'Only what I chased.
    Dust in a hundred cities

and the blind swaying just right.
Mother hanging sheets by the steaming tub.
The bluing smell for my father's shirts.
His white Sunday strolling suit.
His never being dead enough.'

But did you mention the white rooms near Clairmont
or the black roses by the stone?
    'No, only my first bus to Demming, Texas.'

Then it must be time for you to go.

His heels click against the street as he searches for you.

3.

Do you like it this way?
Do you do it often?
Do you like the blind swaying
and the washstand and the cough
in the halls before night?
Do you like the lice-ridden pigeons
cooing their terrible vision of the wino's city?
Do you like the trembling Sunday streets and one café?
Do you like my fat body catching breath?
Do you like our sleep filling the room?
Can you stay this way a little longer
before your bus to L.A.?

He looks in the dirty movies but you're not there.

4.

The cause of death:
These white rooms await the writhing of your life,
well worn and empty.

You enter the echoes
and begin notes on the highway,
the old pickup toward Burntwater
carrying the battered suitcase.

And the poem stops there finally and forever
in the long shadows of the chair
amid the faucets and kitchen smells
where silence is larger than
the room in which you write your life.

It no longer matters that he knows your address.

5.

After the last well-saved valium
you do not remember forgiving yourself
in the vomit and urine
but trying to focus on the spreading dahlias
above the bed.

6.

The man in leather is finally at your bed.
He strips down to your mother
who wanders through your cold boyhood house
giving out blankets to empty rooms.

A wheel in you forgets to breathe,
and you are dead,
and you know you are dead.

7.

Embalmer's report:
He looked like corroded alabaster on the worktable.
His old body, the cracked desert roads, older
than the courthouse square, older than the farmers
spitting their phlegm-filled days,
older than the dirty magazines in the dirty shops
in the dirty cities he so revered.

His open arteries discharged two white colts.
His childless loins repaid
the turquoise, the amber and agate.

His yellowed body finished with the flutes,
finished with the mycins of regret,
finished with the vaporizers and failures,
canceled the bromides and small dreams.
But his eyes wouldn't film
or close, saw further than they should.
Only the two colts remained,
their eyes toward still water,
the blue grass and bean blossom.

8.

What goes into heaven with you
so perfectly prepared on the pillow
like a dead satyr?
Lights from the remaining colts
or the cold cafés of November
near your turquoise hands?
The faceless loins?
The rotted coyotes?
The aged owls?
Agate temple?
Corn fire?

None.

You go without streets, songs, or hair.

9.

Here at the Del Rio, honey
your shaken steps are voided.
An anonymous patron has picked up your tab.
Your room's off the veranda.
It's quiet here except for weekends
when Reba brings the girls down for the sailors.

You look quite young in your famous blue button-down.
A sax and piano begin the waltz.
Sweet Chocolate sends you your first drink.
The neon lights up tit-pink:
   and the night
   and the night
   and the night!

SKIN MOVERS

How still we are in sleep
as though morning holds its breath.
Our bodies rinsed with light
like soaked birch.

Half awake I travel down you again.
Crow, dark crow, we smell of burnt leaves and wine,
the night before taking crystals bitter as Jesuit Root.
Now we turn slowly in the weight of love,
the way ships move heavily between moon and sun, not lost
but like a well-piloted dream.

You speak of a river near home named Dancer's Run,
almost dust in summer that tells the story of the village.
I know your body so and kiss the star mole on your back.
Wanting more, you say yes in that miraculous way.

In this joyous season I know my heart won't die
as you and the milk pods open their centers
like a first snow in its perfection of light.

Good love is like this.
Even the smell of baked bread won't make it better,
this being out of myself for awhile.

OVERWEIGHT

Cooking for someone can be loaded with danger.
He'll get here at six and I'm filled with a small fear
of conversation at the table.
I always toy with the edge across my throat,
between the cabbage, the duck and coffee we stare into.

There are many ways to scream.
I've chosen the silent one
because I'm afraid of being discovered as I am, not
who he remembers 20 years ago.

I want to say things have changed since then.
I've smoked my lungs black and eaten my heart out.
Lost each leaf of hair and seen friends to their graves.

So the real talk is never said.
After a polite time he leaves a bit early.
I want to re-run the dinner again
with simpler food, the apartment a little messy.
I'd like to walk right over the edge and say,
'Who we were then is fable.'
But that takes believing we're someone right now.

Instead I sit down to a second meal.
I'm famished from things left unsaid,
go to bed too early, and wake totally
at the national anthem, before the TV hisses
into blue snow.

I get up. I eat again.

POEMS OF SUBMISSION

1. Submission to Time

How beautiful we are when submitted fully to time,
knowing some tree from childhood crashing then to earth.
Time, the land history found in our pulse.
Land and tree rise like a woman's laughter in a bar.

See the filthy windows.
It's three in the afternoon and we are
drawn from all our fiber.
Three o'clock and the coffee's old.
A chill across our backs.

Now the tenement ages
against the paling sun across the way.
Watch the evening news.
Don't eat so much salt.
See the old man's dog,
the wind-filled street and splitting elm
from such a timeless place.

2. Submission to Pain

Yanis, my friend in the next bed cries:
tomorrow they'll cut his frozen fingers off.
He has submitted that his hands
will never know gathered dust
or circle the chipped edge of a yellow bowl,
even the perfunctory need to touch his penis.
Never to play by fingertip the lyre
of his wife's hair
or draw around slowly her nipples
into rings of heat.

Yanis, Hungarian born, fought in the '56 revolt.
The Russians left holes through which he stares
long out the hospital window:
a mother, grandmother and father.

We prowl the ward late at night
before the Percodan works.
Pretty high once, he told me in Budapest
everything becomes blue with the moon,
that it was not uncommon to see old blue horses
by his house when he was a boy.

Then he apologized,
said the narcotic made his mind odd,
odd like a poet's.

3. Submission to Death

Our loved ones, allowing them to die forever
like noticing the weakened sun in late winter.
Sometimes we let them go through dreams,
giving away their clothes,
keeping only the pocket knife or star quilt.

'Do what you have to,' we remember them saying.
And so we must do with them
who are tired from their effort to be dead,
still not sure where to go,
so they linger with us awhile
before their journey.

Sometimes we sleep well in the midst of terrible grief
or remember something funny they said.
They give these small gifts to us before they leave.
Then for no reason, months later,
we walk into a room unexpectedly filled with flowers
and cry totally, knowing they are dead and forever.

It's good.
Our weeping lessens their memory of us
and they begin to travel more easily,
doing their work, which is to be dead,
not for us or anyone.
We feel better just speaking
of the past,
that too without them.

4. Submission to Single Rooms

The bedroom hovers at dusk
simple as a child practicing piano.
It's summer.
I lie naked on the rose chenille and smoke.

The first time we drank a little whiskey
before our shadow show
ignited like flint sparks.

In the photo on the vanity my mother
looks amazingly young.
I break my vow and think of you often.
Why I left. Because pain rose above us
seeking its own level like a water table.

5. Submission to Silence

How terrible to say nothing,
like an old woman undressing.

It's a stone turned tumor,
more silent than dead meat in a butcher's window,
or a shoe repair filled with the worn gloves of feet.
And sometimes we drive through the white space of sand
noticing the blue line of water clean as opened wrists.

I fry pork for supper.
We sit across from each other,
eating in the silence.

SYPHILIS PRIOR TO PENICILLIN

The United States Coast Guard had a
hospital for it in New York until 1952.
My doctor said if you knew syphilis,
you knew medicine because it
perfectly imitated other diseases.
That in the last stages when it went rampant,
(besides their minds)
sailors would lose a nose or ear,
the disease mimicking leprosy.
And it was never cured or stabilized
so the sailors carried themselves as
weapons into every port.

The whores could never really tell either
for they were eaten with it too.
Those who knew their condition
often banded together
trying not to infect others with
a 'taste for the mud' as the French say.

They were a cavalier and doomed lot,
trying to hold back the dawn
in their foreign hotels,
where the night porters filled rooms
with verbena and gardenias
to hide the cooking smells of sulphur ointments.

At the last there were signs they couldn't hide.
The motor nerves giving way so they walked with
odd flickering steps. That's why Amelia and Rose Montana
would sit the evening through playing mah-jongg,
and the old sailors, Paul and James,
rarely asked the whores to dance.

for DAVID WOJAHN

OSHI

Oshi has a very large Buddha in him, one that can change the air into scented flowers. He used to be Tommy Whalen from Indianapolis but he had his eyes cut to look Japanese. He got started out in San Francisco in the early days when Buddha consciousness was just rising out there and people were still slipping pork in the seaweed soup.

At seventeen he did drag in a place called The Gay Deceiver and was billed as 'The Boy With The Face Like The Girl Next Door.' The owners paid him almost nothing and kept him strung out on hash in a little room above the bar, like a bad detective novel.

Somehow Oshi found the Zen community and started sitting za-zen. He collected 'mad money' from the state for being strung out. It's free out there if you're crazy enough. Oshi breathed hash and gin through the Buddha. Buddha breathed light and air through Oshi. It all changed his mind to indigo. Buddha consciousness rose in him until he didn't feel like the broken piano at the bar anymore.

Now thirty years later he has a permanent room at the bath house and prays for young boys. Doesn't sit anymore. Said he became realized ten years ago with a young hustler from Akron, Ohio who told him he could stop flying, just lay back and touch ground.

Old Oshi, very round now, jet black wig, looks like a retired Buddha in his cheap wash-and-wear kimonos.

He's a graceful old gentleman Buddha. Buys every-one drinks. Gives away joints. Always high. Always lighting joss sticks. As he says, 'Giving things is just a way of getting on with everyone, you know, the universe and everything. It's like passing on the light.'

He told me once when he sang Billie Holliday's 'Blue Monday' at The Gay Deceiver they used an amber spot and he wore a strapless lamé gown, beaded his eyelashes, lacquered his nails, and the people cried.

RETURNING

Ruth, how noticeably you've aged,
the stroke leaving a medical patch
over your left eye.

I visit and you notice me slightly,
staring mostly at old re-runs,
or perhaps thinking of a man named Irving
who's driven up from the Dells for the past 20 years
to engage you both
in what you once were.

Some quiz show starts and
it's the only time you look right at me.
'Do you watch this one? It's good.'
The room's blued by TV.
A late August night, close as sulphur.
Everything's overripe,
the vacation where I stay too long
with old friends who liked me better
the way I was.

She dozes.
I remember her ancient name means compassion.
Ruth, who has gathered herself among sorrow
so quietly she refuses to touch this world again.

I leave the blue and camphor smells,
still hearing the TV in the distance.
Everything falls like slate gray swans in the night,
with asters burning to what's not there.

SUNDAY SNOW

I walk around the cold rooms trying to remember
if it's sorrow or light that brings me to her small face
and ribs I want to play like forbidden chimes.
I walk the cold alone and admit it's sorrow
that brings me to the light.

My emptiness festers into a Sunday forever.
I want to believe in the little girl
beyond my needs for darkness.
I want to bring her into light like a tablet washed by sun,
where she can finger up each contour of my despair.

A gray mist comes from the gray park below as I write:
'A gray mist comes from the gray park below.
The little girl rides a naked horse gray,
rides blood red over his back
in the gray park, in the gray naked snow.'

It is Sunday.
It is Sunday forever and begins to snow.
I am going into the snow
as I have wanted to do for years.

A COLORED GIRL

Me waiting on a bus.
She comes down the street nearly dark,
plum colored taffeta dress, ruffled top,
the way a light wind does on a hot night.

She stops by me, very, very high.
I'm nervous because I think
she's trying to hustle me,
so I ask her for a smoke.
She says sure,
asks if I'm interested in some fun.
I say I'm Gay.
She's lost complete interest and
is digging in this huge bag for a smoke.
Pulls out a bent Salem and even lights it for me.

I ask her how's work.
She says slow on the southside.
I look close at her,
scared because she's so beautiful and made up,
rouge, marcelled hair, nail polish,
and finally say,
'You look like a colored girl.'
She laughs and says,
'I know baby, johns your age like that.'
She walks on and I say, 'Be careful now, hear?'

for B.R.L.

DYING OUT

I love the cambric night snowing down First Avenue
and the heaven of being near things I know,
my apartment, the old rugs and chair, the moons
of my nails above which I write.

And the snow in distant woods where animals
give silently all
and everything into dying—their fossils in spring,
the jonquil and pure bone.

I'm no more alone than usual
with this perfect history of snowing
so quietly without people.
I've left so many this year
who've felt too comfortable with my old design.
Because I want another life rinsed new in middle age,
the way a hard sickness changes a person.
The way snow changes the billboards
by my drugstore to read VANQUISH PAIN and
RELIEF FROM THE ORDINARY.

I don't want forgiveness from people,
only to be seen from another way,
like the back of a sculpture,
perhaps the nape of a neck or an open helpless palm,
some familiar form viewed from another direction.

VINEGAR

In his underwear
a man writes a poem in a motel room
then holds it to a mirror.
The poem begins to translate:
'. . . an oyster white cup on the ebony sill . . .'
Then he writes 'vinegar' and 'old' and begins to cry.

Having matched these objects with something unnamed
the way a smouldering fire can sometimes tell us
who we are, he continues.
The towel and the cup and everything else he sees
burn in vinegar
like the edge of himself.

He dozes at the desk
and dreams of living without danger
or the fear of death.
Dreams of a laundry room in summer
with its cool bleach smell, hands lifting
in Fels Naphtha.
A bowl of bluing . . . simple enough
as though heaven could be so.

A car sounds somewhere and he wakes
nearly dreaming of a Black neighborhood
where a barber chair sits in a front yard,
and a train almost runs through someone's house
by Estelle's Café and Beauty Parlour.

THE ARC-WELDER'S BLUE

Only silence can make it all,
a blue towel, vinegar, and salt fire.
Silence toward totality,
the way giant turtles sum themselves up at death,
going from what they were into the sea,
their claws scratching RUTH and HARROW
on the sand.

Words from silence so excellent at genesis
like a sexual flower,
come through an ill-formed life
where no metaphor of soaring bird will do,
only a coal yard in late sun blazed on black rock.

If silence is possible
it forges the arc-welder's blue
for the corporeal and daily
so we look away and are still drawn.
Silence, submission to the ordinary,
like a memory of a laundry room in summer,
chartreuse light and bluing smell, mingling
with coffee upstairs and more, but distant
and childish, gone.

NAMING

Old woman, my mother,
let's do the world again you and me,
this time in the desert outside Gallup, New Mexico
where the sky's as bright as cut ribbons.

We'd take long walks in our clay life
where nothing's taught and I'd learn everything,
like stopping the wind
by pinning a small shell in your hair, that certain
days in spring are called
mother-in-law weather.
Here is a weed to smoke for dreams
and that's called 'hawk,'
a flutter from the canyon rim.

Old woman, don't die.
Take me to your first words again,
to say there are plants that live as people,
that certain animals carry dreams,
that the hawk is itself where the canyon drops to air.

'Look son, there's a word for getting
off work late at night, your collar
damp with sweat, and one
for loneliness that starts at the base of the spine.
There's a word for mystery,
the morning rose on the kitchen table
opening all on its own,
almost green at the base of the bud,
quietly doing the way it knows to.'

Old woman, my mother,
so full of sickness it becomes acquaintance,
don't die. The world is nearly empty for me.
Take me near your river of first words again.
'Look son, this is stone.
Here is flower.
Here between my legs you entered the world.
Call it "door."
Look son, another flower called going away, and this
is called too soon.'

for MARIE WHITE

James White was born in Indianapolis, Indiana in 1936. At the age of 16 he began his training as a classical ballet dancer and was awarded a scholarship to the American Ballet Theater School. He then danced for ten years in America and Germany.

After his dance career he attended universities in Indiana and Colorado and took two degrees in English Literature. He then went to New Mexico and Arizona to live and teach with Navaho people.

He was brought to Minnesota to develop a creative writing program for Chippewa children through the Minnesota Writers in the Schools Program. He edited two books of contemporary Native American poetry for *Dacotah Territory*, and remained closely affiliated with tribal people.

The Salt Ecstasies is James White's fourth book of poetry. In 1978 he was awarded the Bush Foundation Fellowship for Poetry. He lived alone and taught privately in Minneapolis until his death in July, 1981.

COLOPHON

This book was designed by Graywolf Press and printed and bound by Thomson-Shore in Dexter, Michigan. The typeface is Aldus, designed by Hermann Zapf. Type was set by Irish Setter, Portland, Oregon.